THE NEW LIFE

THE NEW LIFE

POEMS
WALLY SWIST

Plinth Books
WEST HARTFORD, CONNECTICUT

Copyright © 1998 by Wally Swist

All rights reserved.

Manufactured in the United States of America.
Printed on acid-free paper.

Direct all inquiries to the publisher:

PLINTH BOOKS
P. O. Box 271118
West Hartford, CT 06127-1118

FIRST EDITION

Library of Congress Catalog Card Number:
97-69739

ISBN 1-887628-07-X (cloth)
1-887628-06-1 (paper)

Cover Art: untitled watercolor by Richard Yarde

Author photo: Gordon Daniels

Cover and interior design: Charles Casey Martin

Grateful acknowledgment is made to Penguin Ltd. for permission to quote from *The Upanishads*, translated by Juan Mascaró, copyright © 1965 by Juan Mascaró. Reprinted by permission of Penquin Ltd.

*for my parents,
Julia and Ferdinand*

ACKNOWLEDGMENTS

Appalachia: "Catalpa," "Cushman Brook," "Whitetails"
Earth First: "The City of Nails"
Longhouse: "Why We Have Names"
Lungfish Review: "Dogwood"
Northern New England Review: "Tracks of Deer"
Old Crow: "Before Dawn," "Elegy," "The Voice"
Optimist: "My Friends, the Bees," "Rats in the Barn," "Small Miracles"
Osiris: "August," "Coyotes," "Inheritance," "Returning Back To My Body," "Shells"
Outerbridge: "After Putting My Dog Down," "Helping Hands," "The Red Fox," "Whiskey," "Witch-hazel"
Painted Bride Quarterly: "Sweet Woodruff"
Peregrine: "The Light"
Poetry East: "The Bookdealer's Breakdown," "Euterpe Singing," "Setting Type"
Potato Eyes: "The Sudden Nearness"
Rag Mag: "The Mole," "The Voice"
Sanctuary: "Lustre"
Scree: "Negatives"
The Signal: "A Killer Walks"

Snowy Egret: "Desire," "The Geese," "Walking the Meadow in Autumn"
Yankee: "Hurricane"

"Hurricane" was included in the 1995/1996 *Anthology of Magazine Verse and Yearbook of American Poetry* (Monitor Book Company, Inc., 1997).

"Snow Geese: A Mountain Poem" was issued as a poem-in-a-pamphlet by Andrew Mountain Press (1997).

Some of these poems were previously collected in the following limited edition letterpress volumes published by Adastra Press: *Waking Up the Ducks* (1987) and *For the Dance* (1991).

CONTENTS

• I •

After Reading the *Upanishads* / 3
Ode To Cockcrow / 4
Starflower / 6
Ode To Open Meadow / 8
Dry Ledges / 10
Desire / 13
Witch-hazel / 14
Double Rainbow / 15
Snow Geese: A Mountain Poem / 18
Destinations / 22
The Red Fox / 25
Lustre / 27
Cushman Brook / 28
Dogwood / 29
Catalpa / 31
Returning Back To My Body / 32

• II •

August / 35
Hurricane / 36
Walking the Meadow in Autumn / 37
Whitetails / 38
The Geese / 39
The Mole / 40
The Bookdealer's Breakdown / 41

Elegy / 42
Wolf Hour / 43
The Sudden Nearness / 45
Helping Hands / 47
Before Dawn / 48
After Putting My Dog Down / 49
Rats in the Barn / 50
The Trapped Bird / 52
A Killer Walks / 53
The City of Nails / 54
Sophie / 56

• III •

The Owl / 59
Euterpe Singing / 60
Coyotes / 61
Sweet Woodruff / 62
Setting Type / 63
Inheritance / 64
Shells / 65
Why We Have Names / 66
Whiskey / 67
The Light / 69
Negatives / 70
My Friends, the Bees / 71
Morning Snowfall, Haskins' Meadow / 73
Tracks of Deer / 74
Small Miracles / 75
The Voice / 77

I

After Reading the *Upanishads*

> *When the wise knows that it is through the great*
> *and omnipresent Spirit in us that we are conscious in*
> *waking or in dreaming, then he goes beyond sorrow.*
> —from the Katha Upanishad

All day, I have sat
by the water. Now
it is time to walk
the streets of the island,
my footsteps echoing
over the cobbles,
the town's stone dwellings
streaked with the sky
at dusk. When I speak
with the master
at the hermitage,
he says I am welcome
to stay as long as I like.
Once, before waking,
I heard his voice
call my name, ringing
deep within me,
vibrating like a bell,
spreading out like ripples
clear across the water
in the bright morning

Ode To Cockcrow

Rooster,
you awaken me
every morning
to remind me
that I must
start my day.

You project
the scratchy tenor
of your voice,
on whose
squeaking hinges
doors open
to the new life.

Rooster, you awaken
the world,
and as sunlight
begins to stream
through the leaves
down the mountain,
I rise from my bed
in a house
at the bottom
of the hill
and go to work,

my dreams
still moist
with the dew
from the night before.

Rooster, you call
the morning light,
the light that illumines
a new beginning,
and even in gray weather,
even in the rain
of sleet
thundering over
the shed's corrugated
tin roof,
it is your voice, friend,
that rings out
with the affirmation
of the possibility
of weathering
any storm.

Starflower

Star
of the upland woodlands,
seven-petaled,
not unlike the Pleides'
seven sisters,
that speckles
the new green
of the undergrowth
beside the loose talus
of the trail
like flecks of sea foam
amid a bed
of browned pine needles,
springing out of
a whorl of leaves.
Wherever you bloom,
starflower,
your china white
blazes as if
it were fixed
like a pattern
of seven-pointed
starlight,
your petals set
like a constellation

against the shade
spread along
the mountain path
every May.
I see
you everywhere
since now
I know your name.

Ode To Open Meadow

This is where
wildflowers and winds
blossom and end,
verdure bordered
by stone walls,
whose track,
worn by farm wagons
piled high
with bales of hay,
rises and disappears
in morning fog.

It is content to be:
scent of cedar
and scrub juniper,
glimmer of
stone outcrops,
sulphurs wind
a trail between
that patch
of purple clover
and those shoals
of anemones,
then alight upon
each marsh buttercup
dotting the bluestems.

I am cleansed
in watching
the quiet ways
of the foraging
spotted doe,
and how swallows
pluck gnats
from a cloud
that expands
and contracts
beneath Venus
and the crescent,
as if I had died
somewhere along
one of its paths,
and had entered
the bardo,
that time
of blessing
for the soul

in between lives.

Dry Ledges

What is uncanny is the strength
that accompanies the autumn,
as in the oiled chirping
of a cricket penetrating
the diminishing ratchet of cicadas,

or the honking of geese,
that reminds me that fires
still burn in my heart,
as they write themselves
across the smoky sky
in brant,

or the sound of the rain
igniting in the maple's crown
that pulls me into
the gravity of a falling leaf,

and these dry ledges
of the mountain stream,
darkening in the rain,
brightened by a flurry
of blowing beech leaves.

*

That uncanny strength
is what accompanies the autumn—
my skin prickling
from the balm of silence,
ringing like crystal
through the open window
after the drenching
all-night rain,

and the woods
this time of the year,
as each tree spreads
a new bed of leaves,
take on the effect
of a mottled reflection,

the woods
this time of the year
acquire a luminous quality
of light
in hues of yellow,
orange, and crimson.

*

The strength
that accompanies the autumn
is what is uncanny,
but these indentations
that resemble footprints
in the dark volcanic rock,

as if God had walked
up what is now a streambed
while it was still molten,

is the strength that carries me,

as if my soul
flowed with the first silver trickle
of autumn rain.

Desire

All summer, vines and bramble
block the path to the brook.
Black snakes slide through the weeds.
From here, I can see the light
shine on the field of corn stubble
that stretches across the flats.
I beat back briers
and tangles of nettles
beneath the grove of sumac
choked with a new growth of alders.
A startled pheasant flies up.
Feathers float in a cloud of dust,
coyote and raccoon tracks
sunk deep in the mud.
Each year more trees have fallen.
I toss what I can out of the way;
sometimes a rotted trunk
breaks in my arms.
The brook runs high and fast
from the autumn rains
and pounds over the stones.
If I stop to listen I hear
the wind snap a branch of white pine,
deer browse in the grass.
I find myself going further, further.

Witch-hazel

for Rachel

Walking with you on the trail
through the sunlight
slanting over the meadow,
disappearing and reappearing
through the trees,
never the same twice,
but never more radiant
than the light beneath
the delicate bones of your face,
and your laughter warming
this September morning,
as you hold a yellow leaf
from the tree named witch-hazel,
as we hold each other
close once near noon,
the fields still moist with dew,
and the scent of autumn's decay
beginning to burn like a wick
near the shoulders of the pond,
and the blowing mist flaring
across the face of the ridge
singed burnt orange and crimson,
as I hold the memory
of the meadow warm with your laughter,
and in holding this close, protect it
like a sparrow cupped in a child's palms
that turns his entire being into song.

Double Rainbow

Walking the meadow track
after a day of rain,

to what we thought
was the dripping

autumnal incandescence
of trailside maples and oaks,

was, instead, the finest mist
still descending,

the last of the light,
turning it golden

like a shower
of tamarack needles.

Only our angels know
why we stopped to look around

into the sky above the house
to see the spreading prismed arc

broadening its hues,
each clearly distinguished

in three-dimensional bands.
Then, as if reflecting itself,

another appeared above it,
deepening both across the sky

like flames. We stood
beneath it and watched

the colors fade, each
highlighting the other,

making me realize that
we are constantly reawakened

by the wealth of the continuum,
that what we are now

is what we always have been
all the time,

that we were not meant
to be too happy,

but we have grown
into one another,

walking as far as
the hip deep swale,

both of us ionized,
almost hovering there a moment.

Snow Geese: A Mountain Poem

It is not the body
that lasts,
but the memories
of the body—
its consciousness,
the source
at the mountain's summit
rimmed blue with sky.

I want to share
all that I have
with you: my body,
the trail
up the mountain,
the wood asters
beside it,
the marsh hawk
shadowing the trail,
my kisses
warming you
in the rain.

All my life
people have told me
to go away,

and you tell me
if I need you
that you are here.

    *

I walk the old roads
through these hills,
as if for the first time:

the pumpkin fields plowed under,
the sloping valley
cloaked in a shroud of smoke,

still rustling with
an abundance of crepuscular leaves
scoured and scoured
again in the wind...

out of my head with joy.

    *

Why do I believe I knew you
before you existed?

Shimmering dew.
Riderless galloping horse.
Corn tassle.

Ridge after ridge
of rust red
maples and oaks
lulled into creaking
after a surge
of the wind.

The brush ticking with
the inimitable song
of the nuthatch
and white-throated sparrow.

This road
through the late October hills.

*

Years from now,
when we are gone
people will sense
and palpably perceive
the possibility that
someone walked here hand in hand

through a bright trail of beech leaves
scuttling from berm to berm,

and picture,
shadow after shadow,
the flock of migrating snow geese

passing through us.

▣ Destinations

    1.

We're in such a hurry
  that we miss
    our real destinations,
  observe

that flock of pigeons
  along the way,
    roosting on
      a flat roof

pebbled with
  white stones,
    cooing happily
      in the late warmth

of the low November sun,
  beyond which lies
    the river,
      and its reflection,

throbbing
  as it flows,
    before it empties
      into the sea.

2.

We need to remember
　to return
　　to the source,
　　　whose center

can be referenced
　anywhere, blessed
　　by the name
　　　beyond names,

transcribed by us
　through each act,
　　our auras pulsing,
　　　as in knowing

when one has
　finally arrived,
　　crouched among
　　　the stones,

hiking
　snowy mountain,
　　the stream
　　　having drawn us

off the trail,
  as if the light
    were a sound
      rushing in our ears.

The Red Fox

I am sure of the tracks
this morning in new snow
that veer off the meadow path
past the conical stumps
bordering the edge of young willows
and angle towards the beaver lodge
beyond the dogleg of the brook
from which a cloud of steam drifts
downstream heading south.
Doubling back out of the grove
I lose sense of its direction,
but as I look up, I see the fox
there in the meadow,
high-stepping in the snow,
moving with stealth
to study the ground
as if it follows mouse tracks
between snow tunnels.
It does not see me,
until it stops just ten yards away,
and I cease breathing
as it lifts its head, eyes wide
and as bright as black agates,
the hue of its coat
ecstatic in the sunlight,

and for an instant
we are locked in stillness
before it streaks
past birch and poplar
and into a thicket of white pine
to disappear so quickly
it leaves a tint
that lingers like breath
on the cold morning air.

Lustre

The sky tonight,
beginning to blossom with
constellations of spring,
forces me to stop after work
on the walk that glitters
with particles of icicles
shattered by the fall
from the steep pitch
of the shingled roof
the same way the sparkle
ignited in the eyes
of that herd of deer,
frozen in headlight beams
for only an instant,
in the first blizzard
of winter, crossing the road,
quietly, with such modesty,
that they softened
the wild falling of the snow,
and how we reached over
to the other in the darkness,
how our hands found
the shape of touch,
as if we held the lustre
infused in their starry eyes.

Cushman Brook

A kingfisher chatters
in the willow, plovers cry,

the blue tips of reeds
emerge from the surface

of the emerald green pond,
the meadow glistens

in pools of melting snow,
fallen late, last night.

Above me geese pass
in a strong northwest wind.

If coolness has a sound,
the brook's roar lifting

past the grove of alders
is that sound.

Dogwood

Whose flowers
　seem to float
　　along its limbs,
　　　as a mobile

placed in the air,
　as delicate as the word
　　for slenderness,
　　　hosomi, in Japanese.

Whose petals
　bear the imprint
　　of the red rimmed
　　　lipstick kiss

of the princess
　of blossoming trees.
　　Whose suchness evokes
　　　the exclamation, "ah."

Whose blown blossoms
　become a small rain,
　　conjuring Lao Tzu,
　　　who lectured

   beneath it about
     Tao, and suggested
       the middle path
         can be found

in the calligraphy
 of dogwood petals
   as they write themselves
     on a page of the wind.

Catalpa

This is what succulence is:
the trumpets of your blossoms
spilled across the path,

the centers of their white funnels
striped orange and spotted purple.
Inhaling their fragrance,

I am unaware of the source,
until I find myself standing beneath you.
As a trail of fallen petals

disappears into the swale,
you broad heart shaped leaves,
rocking from the branches

of your massive crown,
send a shudder through me
in the sudden coolness of this rain.

Returning Back To My Body

I awaken
to the light
that shines
on the surface
of the water
I rise towards
and break.

II

August

The sky rips open
after days of grinding heat,
waves of meadow grass
shift in the blowing rain,
and floating on the breadth
of its extended wings,
as bright as a vision,
the great blue heron
strokes through the storm.

Hurricane

The shutters applaud themselves
with lunatic frenzy. Their hinges
have swallowed their tongues.

A weatherman's voice fizzles
in a gasp of static. The wind
lifts fists of stone.

Shingles are stripped, windows
go blind, and all the echoes
clench their teeth.

As you light the candles,
lightning brushing our shadows
splinters like glass.

Walking the Meadow in Autumn

Withered flowers of goldenrod
rock in the wind, silver with frost.

A porcupine plods through the brush,
emerges, retreats,

quills raised and quivering.
Grass, trampled beneath

the barbed wire fence,
stirs, where, more than once,

I have seen a dark shape
slip away at dusk.

A marsh hawk circles, riding an updraft.
Thistle seeds sail the air.

Whitetails

Turning my head
 at the crack
  of a fallen branch,

"whitetails," I say,
 spotting two does.
  They bound away

into the sedge,
 and zigzag
  over the hummocks,

the undersides
 of their tail patches
  silky-tufted

like open milkweed pods.
 In mid-leap, suspended,
  they vanish

into the fallen dusk
 already glittering
  with early frost.

The Geese

Wedge after wedge
have flown over the ridge
in great waves wheeling south.

But, tonight, geese
cut off from their flock
pass close above my head
in thick fog.

I lift up my voice
in song, and call to them
by way of greeting.

I am surprised when they begin
to follow me toward the glare
showered from the spotlight
on the side of the barn.

Each one answers
the trumpeting of the other
and my singing,
as they circle in the light,
before they regroup
to continue their journey.

Once again, alone, now in the silence,
I am filled with their voices.

The Mole

Your eyes are vestigial,
not unlike a visionary's,
one who went blind,
and withdrew deeper
and deeper into a privacy
never remote enough.

Often, in spring, rills
of your tunnels
cross the meadow
during heavy rains
in the wet ground.

Your feet
are shaped like
small shovels;
even your nose
looks like a tuber.

Finding you dead
this morning in the grass,
I realize that whatever
was about to happen
has already happened
and that the years
of darkness have
already begun.

The Bookdealer's Breakdown

Sometimes he says
the strangest things to me
in the elevator.

He comes apart
like a loose hinge,
a broken book opening

in the wind
that gusts up the shaft
as we descend—

all those pages
of information riffling
between the floors.

Elegy

Those thoughts
in the middle of the night
that drove you to your death

linger in the darkness
like the traces
of a smoking gun.

If our grief could
carry a tune, the darkness
would hum with it.

Wolf Hour

Dear Sorrow:
you have caught me
genuflecting
as I have walked
from room to room.

You have watched me
kiss the crucifixes
in the house.
You have seen me
bless myself.

Dear Sorrow:
someone has stuck
the kewpie dolls
with pins, and all
the dummies erupt

vocably with
an undignified chatter.
I am punished
by their howls...
by the clock's ticking;

its water torture
of a single thought,
repeating: *you*

*have done nothing
with your life.*

I toss on one side,
then another. And
dear sorrow:
every way I turn,
I am impaled

on nothing's blade.

The Sudden Nearness

Driving to work
in traffic over
the Calvin Coolidge Bridge
I try to stop short
to avoid the car ahead,
and lose the brakes
in the '71 Volkswagen,
then swerve
into the oncoming lane.
Thank God, there are
no cars coming, that
I am quick enough
to pull up
the emergency brake.

I may never have seen
the sunlight again
that falls through
the mountain ash
by the barn in October;
the sudden nearness
after first snow
of the white pine
that fringes the meadow;
the brook's cool surge
that rushes through April,
past budding pussy willow;

not another taste
of farm fat tomatoes,
sweet corn, the trout
I manage to catch.

"This is my life," I think,
"the best of everything,"
and skid to a stop
on the far side of the bridge.

Helping Hands

Some days are worth it.
You make up
with your wife.
Even the boss smiles.
You catch the crystal vase
before it hits the floor.
The trouble with your car
is a loose fan belt
and not the engine.
That pain in your chest
is inexplicably gone.
People's faces brighten
when they see your dog
leaning out
the back seat window,
her ears flapping
in the wind.
For once, you listen
to an inner voice.
It urges you to drive
the long way home.
A goldfinch's song
rings from a nearby tree.
You let your imagination
take you places,
as if helping hands
suddenly become wings.

Before Dawn

for Bert Meyers

Wind turns
and turns again
like a man
in his sleep.

A mouse rummages
in the bureau,
jarring the familiar
and the forgotten
from drawer to drawer.

Birds canvass
about existence;
the alarm clock
buzzes like
a dentist's drill.

The wind's a semi
that's driven
all night
past the poplars.

After Putting My Dog Down

Her blonde Labrador's fur
blends with the shaft
of sunlight I let in
after finally
opening that door
to the room at the vet's
I wailed in.
I leave her as if
she were waiting for me
any Saturday morning—
head on paws,
tail curled
in a wagging abeyance,
patient, as she always was,
so help me, I thought
I could learn that
virtue from her,
always ready
for my call to come,
"Come Cider, let's
go for a walk to the brook."

Rats in the Barn

As O'Keeffe watched
desert snakes crawl
she tried to overcome
the crawling of
her own skin.

Old Earl, storyteller
and itinerant handyman,
had a similar problem
every time he tried
to quit drinking.

My fear was no worse
as I walked to the barn
every morning to gather
brushes, ladders,
and cans of paint,

to feel cold sweat bead
as I listened to the rats
drag themselves across
the warped boards
that floored the hay loft,

to know the shadows
had eyes. Only after
the job was finished

and all the shutters
were rehung

just a day before
first snow, Old Earl
announced he had
shot one in the head,
"big as a cat," he said.

The Trapped Bird

At first I thought it may be
a mouse that gnawed
inside the wall, a heartbeat
in a chest only inches away,
that could be felt
when I touched the place
with my hand.

It could have been a fledgling
fallen from a starling's nest
out of the eaves, backward
into the maze of rotted wood,
whose struggle inside the wall
gave terror a gravity
I had not known.

I listened to it climb
the passageway it descended,
each time rising higher
then sliding back down,
until its voice cracked,
and the scratching
ceased to claw the air.

A Killer Walks

1.

When she leaves for her car in the parking lot,
juggling gifts in one arm to search for keys,
it happens quickly. Everything evil happens fast.
A shadow leaps, ignites a chill,
packages spill across the seat.
In the struggle she is turned upside down,
feet sprawled over the headrest,
faceup beneath the steering wheel.
She is left as if she were being born,
headfirst, out of the bloody womb of this life
into the next.

2.

If we have not grieved for the buffalo,
if we have not grieved for the fish
that no longer spawn in the polluted
waters of the big two-hearted river,
if we have not grieved for this young woman,
we should begin—
because a killer walks
out across the winter asphalt,
and as his pace quickens
he leans into the night,
and slices through the shiver
he leaves in the air.

The City of Nails

Here it is, up ahead, beyond
that hairpin turn where
old values are blacklisted,

where law abides by its own
private pool of sewage
curiously like poor Narcissus,

where death is
the street punk
telling us this

is the arrival, the departure
no one has ever
prepared for enough,

where inverted road signs
map the new archetype
and billboards advertise

wash-and-wear sex,
the most refreshing colas,
totems of refined taste,

where the marriage of anima and animus
is just another one-night stand
for machisma and machismo.

Here it is. Go ahead.
Welcome to the city of nails
where every telephone pole

lining the farthest limits
to the main strip
is condemned for crucifixion.

Bear down. Head on
the dark side unravels
like black crepe.

Sophie

shuffles in the hall
in her slippers.

She speaks to herself
in Polish and in English.

She asks you the time,
and what is for breakfast,

for lunch, and for dinner.
She asks you how you are,

and rarely steps outside.
Years of psychiatric drugs

have made her tongue stick out.
Even after her single mastectomy

she still keeps her money
tied around her neck

in a roll beneath her housecoat,
in the groove between her breasts.

She makes sense of the world.
Sometimes she even sings.

III

The Owl

I am awakened
by cries that do not stop.
They say, come, see if you can find me—
half the meadow in moonlight,
the other half shadowed by white pine.
A pair of eyes fly up and dance,
owl eyes that hold the moon.

Euterpe Singing

Sing for me, I said,
and she did.

Such simple lyrics
she sang to what goes

beyond language.
Teach me, I said,

and she answered,
I will show you

swinging ropes of song,
but you will be able to

hold nothing,
and her voice rose.

Show me, I said,
how to sing,

and put my hands
together in prayer.

Sing for me, she said,
and I did.

Coyotes

Two A.M., howling
begins on the edge
of one of the farms
left in this valley,
near the wetland
a developer has mown.
Such pure sound
pierces the night,
this bloodletting
beneath Orion,
this ghostly choir
of thin cries that tremble
like Shawmut and Massasoit
come back to haunt us.
Then the baying of one hound
sets another hound baying
from the far rim
of the opposite ridge
and porch lights flicker
on the water
of this delirious music
and the wild pack
in each of us
rises into song.

Sweet Woodruff

for Robert Francis

Those slips
of sweet woodruff
you gave as gift
stand in tribute
to our visits.
We brought fruit,
looked up words
you had saved
so they could be
as crystalline as
our friendship
and grounded in trust
like those slips
of sweet woodruff
that have taken root
with an aroma
that permeates
our memory.

Setting Type

for Gary Metras

In a basement pressroom
we set in December cold.
The composing stick
grows heavier, breath
smokes the air.

Breaking
the concentration
that fires
quiet hard work,
we pause—
our fingers
blackened with
printer's ink.

I begin to understand
the sweat this takes,
and love;
feel the impression
handset type leaves
on the page
like a deep kiss.

Inheritance

Simply, what my parents taught
from the first
strokes of the alphabet
practiced in writing tablets,
exemplifying flourishes
of the Palmer method,
a working class ethic,
and books—
that have led me
on long walks
to where the leaves
are sprinkled
with light.

Shells

As she taught the alphabet
my mother collected shells,
mounting polished conchs,
augers, sundials, and whelk
in a glass case on velvet.

As a child, I recited the alphabet
as waves rolled from the sea to land.
I have never lost the words
found in a harbor, the shells
brought home from the beach.

I still pocket them
as I walk the shore
and press some to my ear
so that I can listen again
to the beginning.

Why We Have Names

So we may be recognized
in our scrapbooks.

So we may learn
to depend on ourselves,

even though our angels
are never far.

So we may know
to whom we belong.

So we may be able
to walk in the door

and call out
to someone we love—

it's good to be home.
In daily sufferings,

so we may remember
who we are.

Whiskey

Near the hedges
he watched his father
kill black snakes—

the hoe's edge
sliced thick
writhing coils.

He swallowed a fly,
and his mother went into
the kitchen, returning

with whiskey;
it would kill the germs,
do not tell your father.

He sipped the jigger
in the warm Floridian twilight,
and it radiated within him.

Things grew heavy—
the twilight deepened
in sepia tones,

the swing set
assembled by his father
glowed in amber,

and he shuffled to bed
through the buzz of television
in neighboring houses.

When the story was told,
he expected ire,
the red hot flare

of his father's temper,
those strong hands
pounding the counter top,

but instead, all three
recoiled in unison,
laughing.

The Light

for Barry Sternlieb

We watched the dusk,
saw the faces
of women glow.
The company of men
is powerful.

You wanted
to become the light,
the dusk.
Often we forget
we are just men,

whether we watch
dusk fade,
or are kindled by
faces of women.
The glow is

always beyond us
and only a facet
of one we search for—
the dusk edged hills
calling us home.

Negatives

A friend returns
negatives of photographs
you took of each other
years ago.

You sent the originals
back home to other friends
to show them how well
you were doing.

Now you hold negatives
up to the light
and count what is lost
a frame at a time.

You hold them high
as if you were being robbed.

My Friends, the Bees

for John Maziarz

That first winter night
when you helped untie the mattress
from the top of the car
and we carried it upstairs,
all you said was: "We will
find a river." And with that
I was alerted to the currents
that flowed inside you.
Then into summer
and through fall you held ladders
while I painted tall Victorian peaks
and gripped the shutters
you handed to me,
more than just the stickiness
of paint between us.
You began stories with "well yass,"
and I followed you coon hunting
over expanses of swamp
abundant with pussy willow.
You would punch the time clock
the next morning at the factory,
spent, but full
of the river you had found.
That next spring, at dusk,
when the smell of damp earth rises,
you took me out back
to the abandoned servants' quarters,

only days before a doctor's diagnosis
of cancer, and there
where a broken water pipe
made a right angle
over the blossoming hawthorne
came the dripping from the hive
that first covered your index finger
then flowed over your entire hand
with a buzzing that matched
the quiver in your voice
when you declared,
"My friends, the bees."

Morning Snowfall, Haskins' Meadow

Blowing clouds bury the day moon.
Snow turns the wind white
and fills fox tracks
that lead across
the meadow to the brook.

A towhee calls beyond
ditch stonecrop and burdock
on the path ahead of me
through the hawthorn.

When I walk over
three fallen alders
lying across a gully
of groundpine,
a drumming of wings
explodes out of
a grove of hemlock,

and I lose myself
in the ring
around a pheasant's neck.

Tracks of Deer

When at last the dusk
has collected the darkness,
it gathers
in the wells
and deep troughs.

The moon takes its place
beside the silo's reflection
and a cloud of midges
condenses in the air
above the pond.

On these paths
burnished by wind,
that drop into
the shape of meadow,
I bend down, touch earth.

Small Miracles

1.

I throw scraps of bread
this morning for the birds
in grass I have cut
the night before around the shed—
waist-high grass,
now trimmed to the ground.

2.

I watch the rain stop,
the sky clear in the pond.
I breathe in sheets
of rainwashed air.

3.

Barn swallows,
those dark handkerchiefs,
that drop from the sky
and lift again,
find a place to perch,
then pause on the rim
of a perfect arc.

4.

What I do best is fly
into the eternity of an image
like the cricket,
that black jewel,
who sings about nothing
but this
all night.

5.

Mirrors do not bring
life into focus—
I am just someone
who is losing his hair.
Fields where I walk
turn green every year.

The Voice

I am walking
in a field
of tall grass.

I hear her
call my name.
I am listening

to her voice
in the wind.
She calls me

as if she
spoke to me
from another world.

THE AUTHOR

Gordon Daniels

Wally Swist was born in New Haven, Connecticut in 1953. His essays, poems, and reviews have appeared in such publications as *The American Book Review*, *The Anthology of Magazine Verse and Yearbook of American Poetry*, *Poetry East*, *The Small Press Review*, and *Yankee*. He has published several chapbooks of his work, often in letterpress limited editions, and is the recipient of several awards for his poetry, as well as a grant from the Connecticut Commission on the Arts. He has made his home in rural western Massachusetts for more than fifteen years.